RHS
Garden Bugs

HOW TO USE THIS BOOK

Read the captions in the eight-page booklet and, using the labels beside each sticker, choose the image that best fits in the space available.

•

Extra stickers have been included for you to decorate your own busy garden bugs scene on pages 4–5.

•

Don't forget that your stickers can be stuck down and peeled off again. If you are careful, you can use your *Garden Bugs* stickers more than once.

DK | Penguin Random House

Written and edited by Ben Hoare; Design: Mo Choy, Spencer Holbrook
Picture research: Myriam Megharbi; Production: Claire Pearson

The publisher would like to thank the following for their kind permission to reproduce their photographs:
Abbreviations key: t-top, b-bottom, r-right, l-left, c-centre, a-above, ST-sticker page
2 DK Images: Oxford Scientific Films (tl); **2–3 DK Images**: Natural History Museum, London (insect shapes). **6–7 DK Images**: Natural History Museum, London (insect shapes).
8 DK Images: Natural History Museum, London (insect shapes). **ST1 Alamy Images**: Byron Schumaker (ca). **DK Images**: Colin Keates/Natural History Museum, London (crb);
Frank Greenaway/Natural History Museum, London (cla), (tc), (tr); Natural History Museum, London (c). **ST2 DK Images**: Frank Greenaway/Natural History Museum, London (c);
Jerry Young (tr); Stephen Oliver (tc). **ST3 DK Images**: Colin Keates/Natural History Museum, London (c). **Jacket images**: *Front*: **Alamy Stock Photo**: Byron Schumaker cb;
Dorling Kindersley: Natural History Museum, London crb; *Back*: **Dorling Kindersley**: Natural History Museum, London cra, Jerry Young br.

Published in association with the Royal Horticultural Society (RHS). Royalties from the sale of this book go
towards the charitable work of the RHS, promoting horticulture and helping gardeners. Visit www.rhs.org.uk for more information.

This edition published in 2016
First published in Great Britain in 2006 by Dorling Kindersley Limited
One Embassy Gardens, 8 Viaduct Gardens, London, SW11 7BW

A CIP catalogue record for this book is available from the British Library

ISBN-13: 978-1-4053-1478-7
ISBN-10: 1-4053-1478-8

Colour reproduction by Colourscan, Singapore
Printed and bound in China
Imported into the EEA by Dorling Kindersley Verlag GmbH. Arnulfstr. 124, 80636 Munich, Germany

For the curious
www.dk.com

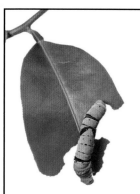

Plant-eaters

An army of small creatures love to eat the plants in your garden. They munch leaves, nibble green shoots, and pick at petals. Some visit flowers to drink the sugary nectar, and a few chomp on wood. How many plant-eaters have you seen?

Hoverfly
Do you think this fly looks like a wasp? That's the idea – it means other animals leave it alone.

Common garden slug
Slugs come out at night to eat juicy green leaves. They slowly slide around, leaving behind a trail of slime.

Peacock butterfly
The spots on the wings of this butterfly look a bit like eyes. They confuse hungry birds that might try to eat it.

Puss moth caterpillar
This strange-looking beast eats the leaves of willow and poplar trees. Finally, it turns into a beautiful moth and flies away.

Green shield bug
The green colours of this bug help it hide among leaves. Its tough body is shaped like a shield.

Orange tip butterfly
Look out for this little butterfly from early summer. Only the males have orange tips to their wings – the females are much more plain.

Brown garden snail
Snails have huge appetites. Nibble-marks on leaves show where they have enjoyed a midnight snack. Many gardeners don't like snails much!

Large white butterfly
This insect flutters around flowerbeds in summer. To get energy, it drinks sweet nectar, so it has a very long tongue to reach into flowers.

Garden tiger moth
Most moths come out at night. This one has bright colours to warn enemies that it tastes horrible.

Honeybee
Worker bees like this one live in nests called hives. Each hive is home to thousands of bees. Inside the hive, they make honey from nectar collected from flowers.

Stag beetles
Male stag beetles have ferocious jaws. They use them to wrestle each other in fights over females. Stag beetle grubs feed on rotting wood and tree roots.

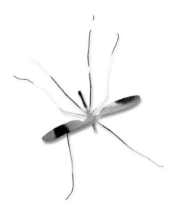

Hummingbird hawkmoth
This moth flies in the daytime and hovers to sip nectar from flowers. As it hovers, its wings beat so fast, it looks like a tiny hummingbird.

Bumblebee
The bumblebee is big and hairy. It flies more slowly than other bees and makes a much louder buzzing noise, too.

Cranefly
These strange flies are also called daddy-long-legs. Their legs are very fragile, so be careful if you touch one.

Cockchafer
This beetle is an excellent flier. It has two pairs of wings and enormous feelers, or antennae. At night it is attracted to bright lights.

Cicada
The cicada is a bug found in warm countries. This one lives in North America. In summer the male produces an incredibly loud buzzing "song".

Large white caterpillars
You'll find these caterpillars in the vegetable patch, where they can do a lot of damage. Their favourite foods are cabbage and other brassicas.

3

PLANT-EATERS

Peacock
butterfly

Common garden slug

Hoverfly

Large white
butterfly

Green
shield bug

Orange tip
butterfly

Cicada

Honeybee

Brown garden snail

Garden tiger moth

Puss moth
caterpillar

Hummingbird hawkmoth

Stag beetles

Cranefly

Cockchafer

Bumblebee

Large white
caterpillars

PREDATORS

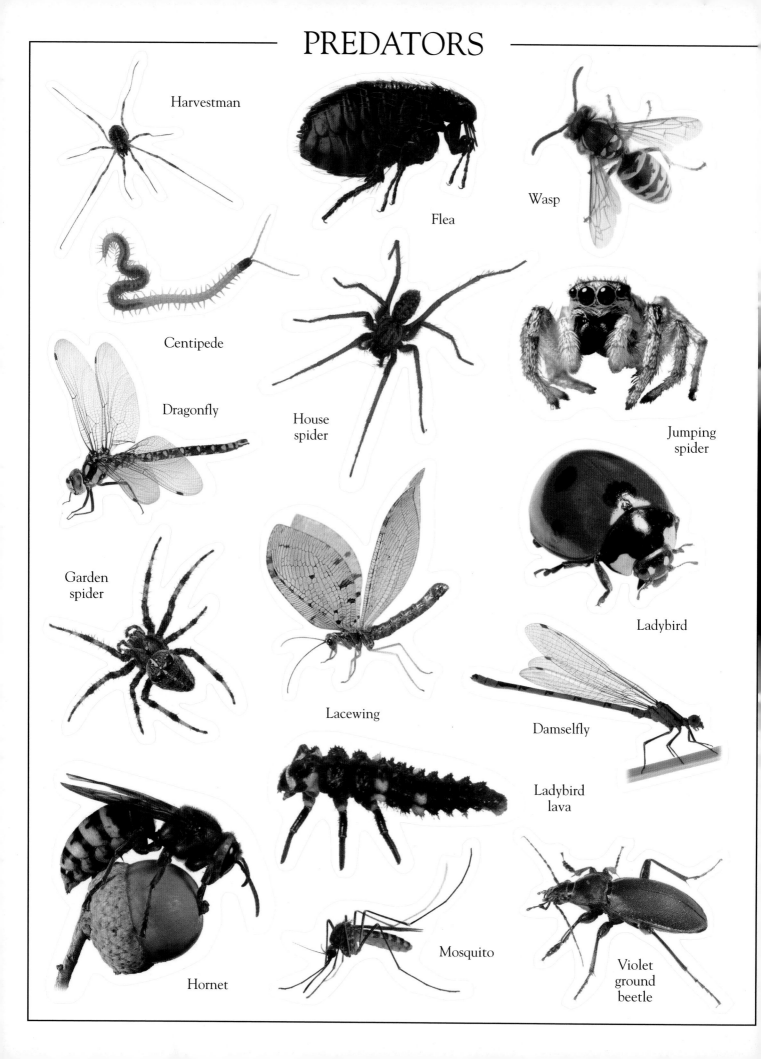

Harvestman

Flea

Wasp

Centipede

Dragonfly

House
spider

Jumping
spider

Garden
spider

Ladybird

Lacewing

Damselfly

Ladybird
lava

Hornet

Mosquito

Violet
ground
beetle

EXTRA STICKERS

Bumblebee

Earthworm

Woodlouse

Centipede

Praying mantis

Jumping spider

Hoverfly

Thorn bug

Caterpillar

Monarch butterfly

Brown garden snail

Housefly

Grasshopper

Rove beetle

Wood ant

Stag beetle

Devil's coach horse beetle

Banded snail

Red admiral butterfly

SCAVENGERS

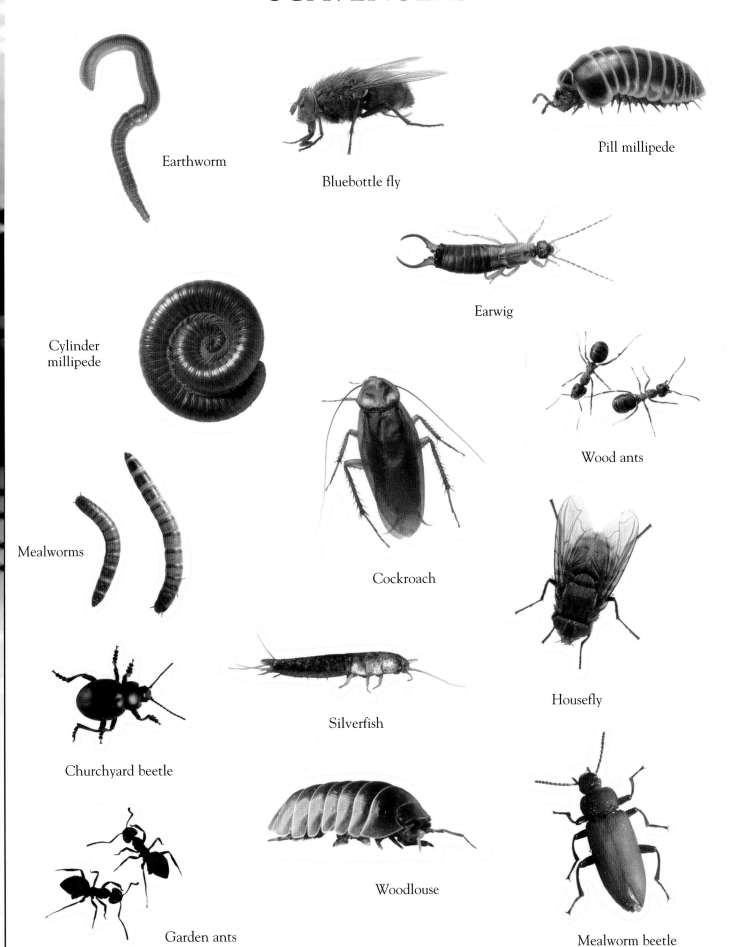

Earthworm

Bluebottle fly

Pill millipede

Earwig

Cylinder
millipede

Wood ants

Mealworms

Cockroach

Housefly

Churchyard beetle

Silverfish

Woodlouse

Garden ants

Mealworm beetle

Predators

Your garden or backyard is full of predators, from hairy spiders to slithery centipedes. Some chase their prey, while others lie in wait to ambush their victims. Blood-suckers can feed from animals without killing them, so are not predators but parasites.

Centipede
A centipede's body has many segments, each with a pair of legs. It twists and turns like a snake, and slips through tiny cracks.

Mosquito
Only female mosquitoes bite. These parasites stab our skin with their sharp mouthparts, then suck up a little blood.

Dragonfly
An expert flier, the dragonfly darts to and fro so fast that it can look like a brilliant flash. Its huge eyes help it spot prey.

Ladybird
This handsome beetle is a ferocious hunter. It eats lots of the greenfly that damage plants, so is very helpful to gardeners. Some ladybirds are yellow or orange.

Lacewing
Look out for lacewings on summer nights. They are named for the delicate pattern of veins on their see-through wings, that look like fine lace.

Garden spider
This is the spider that spins a deadly web of silk to trap flying insects. Spider silk is incredibly sticky and stretchy.

Damselfly
These pretty insects look like small, slender dragonflies. You are most likely to spot them near a pond, because they lay their eggs in water.

Flea
These tiny insects cling
to mammals' fur and birds'
feathers. They suck the
animal's blood, then jump
off to find another victim
to feed from.

Violet ground beetle
During the day, this beetle
hides under logs and stones.
At night it comes out to hunt
other insects, worms, and slugs.

Ladybird larva
This larva, or grub, roams plants
to hunt prey. It pounces on
greenfly, and then uses its strong
jaws to suck their juices. One day,
it will turn into an adult ladybird.

Wasp
A wasp's sting is a weapon
for killing its prey, such as
flies. Wasps also love to
eat sugary nectar and fruit.

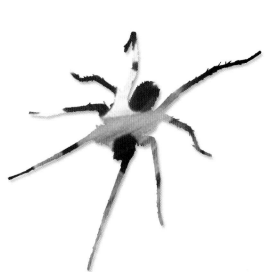

House spider
With their big, long legs and
hairy bodies, house spiders can
look quite scary. You may not like
sharing you home with them, but
they are quite harmless.

Hornet
The hornet is a kind of large wasp.
Like other wasps, it is a social
insect and lives in nests. Each nest
has a queen, who lays the eggs
that hatch into hornet grubs.

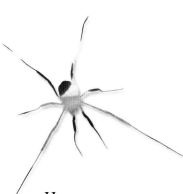

Harvestman
Tiny hooks on the harvestman's
front legs help it to snatch at prey.
It can't bite, but defends itself
from its enemies by squirting a
foul-smelling liquid at them.

Jumping spider
This spider has eight
eyes, and the four at the
front are huge. Its superb
eyesight can detect the
slightest movement. It
does not spin a web, but
leaps onto its victims.

Scavengers

These animals do not eat living plants or kill prey – but almost anything else goes. They eat rotting plants, the dead bodies of other animals, rubbish, and our food. Some even chew clothes!

Pill millipede
The pill millipede's tough, shiny body protects it like a suit of armour.

Garden ants
Ants stay in touch by smell and leave scent trails for other ants to follow.

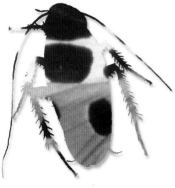

Silverfish
Don't be fooled – this is an insect, not a fish! It scurries across the floor in kitchens, searching for crumbs.

Earwig
The earwig uses its pincers for defence. Male earwigs also pinch each other in battles over females.

Cockroach
These insects are pests in houses, restaurants, and food shops. They eat all kinds of food and rubbish.

Cylinder millipede
If it is attacked, the cylinder millipede quickly rolls up into a tight ball.

Mealworms
These wriggly creatures are mealworm beetle larvae. Fishermen use them as bait.

Earthworm
Worms are tiny earth-eating machines. They absorb nutrients from the soil and pass the rest out the other end.

Churchyard beetle
This beetle lives in sheds and cellars. It munches decaying plants and rotting food.

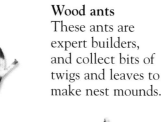

Wood ants
These ants are expert builders, and collect bits of twigs and leaves to make nest mounds.

Bluebottle fly
A bluebottle is very fast and agile in the air. They lay eggs on dead animals, on which their maggots feed.

Woodlouse
Dark, damp places suit the woodlouse. Turn over flowerpots or logs and you might find some hiding.

Housefly
The housefly cannot chew, so it spits on its food, then drinks the soupy mixture.

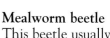

Mealworm beetle
This beetle usually lurks indoors. It feasts on stored flour, grain, and cereal, where it also lays its eggs.